Heavenly Poetry

Heavenly Poetry

Richie Sweitzer

yucky papa ink

If You Feel Alone, You're Not!

I used to feel alone that no one cared about me.

There used to be an emptiness inside of me.

I felt like no one cared about me.

I wanted attention so bad when I was younger that I seeked for it in a negative way.

There was no joy or happiness in my life.

I felt useless inside my heart.

I would think that I am not good enough to be around family or friends.

I was always down, depressed, and unhappy.

Most of the time I isolated myself from others.

I used to feel insecure and uncomfortable.

Remember you are not alone God is with you.

Have You Lost Someone Special?

I had a friend named Pat Postler who was more then a friend to me.

She was more of a mother figure then a friend.

Pat gave me the mothers love I was looking for, for so long.

She was the one person I felt comfortable talking to when something was bothering me.

My mother left me when I was 2 years old.

That made it hard for me to grow up as a child.

Till Pat Postler came into my life.

She was always there for me when I needed her.

Before I graduated high school, she passed away in her sleep.

When I heard the news, it tore my heart into pieces.

Have You Ever Felt Angry?

I always used to be angry.

Why was I so angry?

I don't know why.

I would ask myself, "What am I so mad about?"

I would get mad about everything.

I would always go off about everything.

I have dealt with a lot of drama in my life.

My dad gave me a lot of drama through my life.

I felt like there was no escape from the drama.

Then I learned there was an escape from all the drama.

That is through Jesus.

Strong Fighter!

I have been let down so many times.

Ive been put down so many times.

But I always stood my ground.

Yes I have been through some ups and downs in my life.

But I always stand strong.

There are times where I felt weak.

But I always stood strong.

I may have fallen short, but I've always picked myself up and dusted myself off.

Remember you have the strength to fight your battles.

What is family?

Family are people who care about you.

You may argue with them but they will always love you.

Family can be a group of friends who have known each other for years.

The importance of family is particularly important.

Family comes in many different forms.

You can get support from family with love, forgiveness, and kindness.

Family is always there for you.

So what is family about?

| 6 |

Light/Darkness

Being in the darkness is being under Satan power.

Satan wants to kill and destroy.

God wants to bring you to the light.

He is full of love and mercy.

Satan wants to keep you down and sad.

God wants to lift us up and use us to preach his gospel.

The devil wants to use us for evil.

Do you want to be in light or in the darkness?

What does God mean to me?

God is a spirit full of love and forgiveness.

He forgets all our sins and wrong doings.

The Holy Ghost is slow to anger because he cares about his children.

All who believe in him are a child of God.

We must do what is gods will.

God means hope, joy, and happiness to me.

He is full of peace and happiness.

Have you ever been verbally, mentally, physically abused?

I have been verbally, mentally and physically abused all my life.

There would be times I would think there would be no help at all.

My dad would verbally abuse me daily.

I was getting abused on the daily basis sense the age of 2 years old.

So, if you think help is not on the way it is.

Remember to stay strong because I did.

Seeking for Attention

There would be so many times I was seeking for attention in a negative way.

I was longing for attention so bad I didn't care how I got it.

This emptiness for attention was killing me inside.

The burning inside for attention was eating me up inside and out.

I felt so lost and empty inside.

One of the biggest things I desired as a kid was positive attention that I never got from my dad.

How to forgive

To forgive someone, you must forgive yourself first.

To forgive yourself, you must allow Jesus in your life.

I had a hard time forgiving my parents for a long time.

So, if anyone has done you any evil you need to forgive them.

It may not be easy to forgive them.

God will hold it accountable on you till you do.

So, mom and dad I forgive you for all the pain and hurt you gave me.

What is Christmas about?

Christmas is about the birth of Jesus.

Its not about Santa Claus.

This is the time of the year to spend with friends and family.

You should be thankful for what you have.

This is the time to help the homeless and other people that need help.

We are to serve other not ourselves.

The most important gift you can give someone is love and show them that you care.

Fathers love

A father's love is to make a young boy into a man one day.

The love from a father is to mold and shape a young man.

My dad taught me that your word means a lot.

Dads are tough and sometimes gentle to their kids when they need to be.

Dads are especially important in a child's life at a young age.

Fathers are to make their kids into proper young men or ladies in adult hood.

Mothers Love

A mother's love is easy and gentle.

There love is to comfort you during times of need.

Mothers are more patient then dads are.

There love is special because they give birth to you.

A mother is to set an example for a young lady.

Mothers are gentler than dads are and more understanding too.

They are better listeners then dads are too.

Gods Love

Gods is beyond any love on earth.

God's love is a spiritual love from the heavens.

Gods love is like a fathers/ mothers love together but a lot lot lot more powerful.

He can touch a hardened heart.

The love of god is forgiving all the time to his children.

God's love is the most powerful and strongest love there is.

True soldier

A true soldier is a Christian soldier.

A person of god must go through a lot of change for them to turn their lives around.

They need to accept the help of god.

A soldier fights through all their battles.

They don't give up and say I can't do this anymore.

The soldier is strong and always watching out for the enemy.

They are quick and alert and ready to help really fast.

War

The war I'm talking about is a spiritual war.

Its not an earthly war.

This war is between God and Satan.

Satan once was one of God's angels till he messed up badly.

Then God cast him out of heaven because of that Satan is the father of lies.

That is why there is a spiritual war that has been going on for years.

Evil tongue

The tongue is a powerful little tool.

It can be used for evil or good.

You must be careful with your tongue.

It's a tricky little tool.

The tongue can be used in so many ways.

Our tongue has a lot of taste buds.

Remember our tongues are a powerful tool.

|18|

Healing

Healing is a major big change in a Christians life.

It is important for healing to happen.

Healing is a part of change.

The process of healing is very important.

Healing is a part of making a change in your life.

Remember healing is part of the change in your life.

Sin

Sin equals Satan's independent nature.

The devil tempted Adam and Eve with the tree of good and evil.

He is mad at God for kicking him out of Heaven.

Satan wants to be like god.

He was just an angel nothing else.

Sin came into the world because of the devil's hate towards God.

Perfect Role model

The perfect role model is Jesus Christ.

He shows us how to live and treat others.

Jesus is the only one who can truly teach us how to live truly.

He is an example for living.

Our teacher is Jesus and our lord.

He helps in our time of need.

Being Thankful

What does it mean to be thankful?

You are saying thank you for the gift that you have from God.

Everyone has a special gift that they have been given.

Some one's gift is their own little happy place.

My happy place is when I am writing poetry.

So brother Rome I dedicate this poem to you.

Love

Love is like a flowing river from the heavens.

If you want to love others you have to love yourself.

In order to love yourself you need to accept Jesus as your savior.

Then you can start accepting God's love.

God's love is beyond any love on earth.

Once you learn to love yourself then you can love others.

Hate and Fear

Hate and fear are similar in so many ways.

Hate is like fear.

I used to hate and fear my dad at the same time.

The hate and fear for my dad was really strong.

My dad gave me so much hate and fear.

I can not put it into words.

Peace and Joy

God gives peace and joy into our hearts.

He is full of peace and joy.

Happiness comes from the peace and joy that comes from God.

Peace and joy are characteristics of God.

He gives us peace and joy in our daily lives.

How To Help

How to Help ourselves is through Jesus.

We need to Help ourselves first before we can help others.

We need to except Jesus' help for us to make it in life.

Life is not easy; it is hard.

That is how the world goes and works.

Bad Temper

As a little boy I used to have a bad temper.

My temper was off the charts.

My temper used to be strong.

There would be so many times I would have a temper tantrum as a child.

I continuously had a temper tantrum when I was a little boy.

Anger

What is anger all about?

Anger is another of Satan's tools.

I used to have a lot of anger inside of me.

The devil will try to keep us in our old ways, but God saves us.

God saved me from my self.

I was going in the wrong direction on my own.

If god can save me he can save you.

Friends

Friends are like brothers that fight.

A true friend accepts you for who you are.

They appreciate you for who you are.

You two may fight but you always forgive each other in time.

Friends always have each other's backs all the time.

Hope

What is hope?

Hope is something we get from God.

He give us hope through our faith.

Faith gives us hope in our lives.

Our faith is an important part of walking with God.

God gives us hope every day.

With our faith we have hope.

God's Meal

God's meal is his word.

The more we read his word the better.

It is not about us it is about God.

We need to trust in God for everything.

He will provide for us what we need.

Remember to keep in God's meal everyday.

Love Jesus Christ.

Ocean Waves

Our Thoughts are like an ocean wave.

The thoughts of a person are up and down.

An ocean can be beautiful or ugly.

They could be good or bad thoughts.

It can be peaceful thoughts or noisy.

The ocean wave could be good or evil.

Highway

Our feelings are like a highway.

A highway is fast like our feelings.

The feelings of a human are quick like a highway.

They could be happy, sad, or angry feelings.

The human mind works fast like a highway.

Ships

Our emotions are like ships.

The emotions rock back and forth like ships.

Sometimes ships can be dangerous like our emotions.

Ships can be safe or harmful.

We need to learn how to control our ships.

The ships can be harmful and hurtful of the human mind.

Trust and courage

Trust and courage have similar traits.

With trust you can have courage.

Courage gives you trust.

You need both in yourself.

To have it in others

Trust and courage are especially important in everyday life.

Keep in mind trust and courage come from God.

Battlefield

We all have our own Battlefields.

Each person's battlefield is different.

My battlefield is dealing with my Past.

If you have a battlefield stay strong and fight all the way through.

I am slowly going through my battlefield strongly.

Flowing River

Life is a flowing river that doesn't stop.

True life comes from the Lord God.

He is the way of Life.

Life of the flowing river is continuous with God.

The life is continuous death with the devil.

So do you want true life or fake life.

Which one do you choose?

Walk on the beach

Our imagination is like a walk on the beach.

When I use my imagination, I picture myself on the beach.

I like to think of my imagination as a free spirit.

God gave me a creative imagination to use for good purposes.

What kind of imagination did God give you?

Hurt

Hurt is pain you been through throughout your lifetime.

I have been through a lot of emotional and physical pain.

I have been through pain; you are not alone.

Everyone goes through pain in their lifetime.

This is something that everybody goes through in life.

Fire /Ice

God is fire and Satan is ice.

The fire of God keeps us warm.

Satan ice gives you a cold and hard heart.

I used to be in the ice but now I am in the fire.

Some people are in the middle.

That is not good it is one or the other not both.

Are you in the fire or the ice?

Please say you are in the fire?

What is fun?

Fun is when you feel free from your problems.

Fun for me is singing, dancing, poetry and much more.

Doing something you love and makes you feel good is fun.

Fun is supposed to let the child in you out.

We all have one inside of us so be yourself, and don't let anyone stop you from being you.

Snow

Snow is like a white robe from the heavens.

It is fun to watch the snow fall.

There are so many ways you can enjoy yourself in the snow.

This is another form of water that God has created.

Snow is another way to clean the bottom of your shoes.

I have always loved the snow as a young boy.

Riding your bike in the snow is also fun.

Rain / Ice

Rain is like tears from eyes that come from heaven.

Ice is the same as rain, but it is a frozen version of it.

With ice you can skate onit during the winter.

Rain is fun to dance in when its warm outside.

Walking in the rain is very relaxing and peaceful.

All you need is a rainy day for entertainment.

All you need is a winter day to have some fun on the ice.

Rain and ice are all you need for fun and entertainment.

Sun

The sun is bright and cheerful.

That is the way we should be.

I like to think of myself as the sun.

God is bright and cheerful like a bright sun.

God is bright and cheerful like a bright star in the night sky.

The sun is God and the planets are his servants. The rest of the stars are his angels.

Music

Music is another form of poetry.

Its just poetry with music in the background.

This is another way of meditation.

There are many different types of music.

Everyone has different taste in music.

Music has been around for years.

What kind of music do you listen to?

Gold

Gold is precious like heaven where God is.

There is a finer gold where The Lord is.

The gold on earth is nothing compared to what is in heaven.

Things in heaven are way much better in heaven then on earth.

We will be praising The Lord for eternity.

I can't wait to get to heaven when its my time to go.

Rainbow

A rainbow is a promise from the Lord our God.

He is saying that he will not destroy the earth with a flood ever again.

The rainbow is incredibly beautiful to look at.

Every time after it rains you see a bright colorful rainbow in the sky.

Remember that the rainbow is a gift from The Lord to us.

Lake of Fire

The lake of fire is not a pretty place.

Lake of fire is an unpure fire that is from earth.

This place is dark, and you hear the screaming of lost souls.

The Punishment for the unbelievers is the lake of fire.

That is their own fault for their own eternity.

If you want to go to the lake of fire.

You wont like the burning place you are going to.

Universe

The universe is a mysterious place.

Who knows why?

Only God does.

He created the heavens, earth, and universe.

These planets, stars, and galaxies are amazing in different ways.

There are so many things we cannot see.

Like how the planets and sun are perfectly lined up evenly.

How the earth gravity works.

The sun is so bright.

How the sun works.

There are so many mysterious in the universe.

Planets

Have you ever pictured the planets as bowling?

And the sun as a giant pin?

Well I do see the planets that way.

Its fun to picture it that way.

Thing can be fun if you make it fun.

Or you can picture it as something else.

Any thing you want them to be.

So, try it.

It is fun.

Earth

Earth is a beautiful place.

God created the earth for a reason.

The earth has a lot of different animals.

Man named all the animals on the earth.

There are so many nice places to see on earth.

You have the different seas, rivers, and lakes to see.

Remember that the earths beauty came from God.

Black Hole

A hard heart is like a black hole.

The hard heart is dark and evil.

Having a black hole is not good in a Christian walk.

You need to have an easy heart in a Christian walk.

The black hole is no good to you at all.

It will cause you a lot of grief in your heart.

If you have a hard heart turn it around.

Do it to help yourself.

I did it for myself.

True Bible

The true Bible is God's word.

There is the one and only Bible.

All these other Bibles are fake.

Rest of these Bibles are from the devil.

The King James Bible is one of the real Bibles.

Some of these other Bibles are the real ones.

The rest are the fake ones.

So when you get a Bible, get the true Bible.

Respect

Respect is something you earn.

If you want respect you have to give it.

This is another way to build trust.

Trust is respect in another form.

To have trust you need respect.

Respect is an important lesson in life.

You must have respect for everyone you run into.

Respect is not something you get you earn it.

Prison

The prison I am talking about is a spiritual prison.

Not an earthly prison.

Spiritual prison is totally different.

Satan likes to keep us in bondage.

If you have a lost soul, you are in prison even if you do not know it.

Only Jesus can take you out of spiritual prison.

If you want help, ask Jesus.

Parents

Our parents brought us into the world.

We would not be here if it were not for them.

If you are a bad parent man up.

Parents are supposed to give kids love.

They are supposed to be a role model and an example.

As a parent you must always be there for your children through good and bad.

Do not ever leave your children whatever you do.

Do not even think about doing it at all.

Mature vs. immature

Mature means you are grown up verses being a child that is immature.

Some grown ups are immature just as some young men.

I was one of them.

There has been a lot of immaturity I have seen.

You can be immature and not know it.

Like it was or me.

Are you maturing all by yourself?

Or do you need some help with seeing your maturity?

Because I need help seeing mine.

Do not be afraid to have help seeing it in you.

Waterfall

The water of life is like a spiritual waterfall.

The waterfall is full of living water.

It will never ever stop.

Jesus is our living waterfall.

I have the waterfall inside of me every day.

Do you have the living water inside of you?

Keep the living waterfall in you.

New Year

A new year is a fresh start for us all.

What ever you did last year is history.

God gave us a fresh start.

We have a clean slate now so use it.

With the devil our slates are dirty.

We need a clean one to live right.

It may get dirty, but God will always give us a clean one.

Do not worry about the old dirt God will take care of us.

True Man of God

A true man of God has a strong relationship with God.

He knows him well.

They have a good prayer language.

They are always in the word.

The man of God helps other people out.

They are always listening to God.

They are always focused on God.

So, pastor Kurt I dedicate this poem to you.

Spirit vs. Spirit

The spirit I am talking about is God's spirit not the devil spirit.

God's spirit is full of peace.

The devil spirit is full of anger.

I once was in the devil spirit but now I am in God's spirit.

You can change spirit if you are willing too.

I was willing to.

You can too.

There are good spirits and there are bad spirits.

Which spirit do you have inside?

I have the good spirit inside of me.

Will vs. Will

The wills I am talking about is God's will vs. man's will.

Man is always constantly fighting God's will.

That needs to stop now.

But it will not stop.

I used to fight against God's will.

Are you fighting God's will?

We need to follow God's will instead of fighting it.

Keep in mind God's will equals life.

That man's will equal death.

So, do you want life or death?

Angels vs. Demons

Angels fight for us and demons fight against us.

We are to help the angels of God.

If we do not do what we are supposed to do, we are not helping.

Demons like to use other people for evil.

Angels use us for good.

We are for the angels not the demons.

Angels work for the Lord God.

Demons work for the Devil.

Are you for the angels or the demons?

I am totally for the Angels.

Food

Food can taste great or taste terrible.

Just like spiritual food.

Spiritual food is way better for you.

Natural food helps the natural body.

Spiritual food helps the spiritual body.

A lot of people only want to feed the body but not the spiritual body.

We are to eat both foods to feed both bodies.

Fame

Fame is another word for popularity.

So many people want fame.

Some say I want to be like a movie star.

I want to be a prestigious poet.

But It will not be about the fame.

It will be about helping others.

People let fame get to their head.

My fame is in Jesus our savior.

Remember fame is not everything in life.

Sports

There are different types of sports.

We have basketball, baseball, and many more.

God gave us sports so we may have fun.

We can play them or watch them.

Some people think of sports as a lifestyle.

Others just play them for fun.

I play sports just for the fun.

Some people do it for a living.

Other people just like being on a team.

We all have different tastes in sports and sport teams.

Humor

Humor is another word for laughter.

Humor is the best medicine on earth.

There have been times when I was mad, and someone told me a joke and I felt better.

You can say humor is not medicine, well it is.

It is a feel-good medication that has been around forever.

I love humor a lot.

Humor cracks me up in any mood.

Do you love humor like I do?

School of Jesus

Every true believer is in the school of Jesus.

You get into the school of Jesus by accepting Jesus in your life.

If not you are in the school of Satan.

I once was in the school of Satan, but now I am in the school of Jesus.

A lot of people are in the school of Satan.

I am glad and proud to be in the school of Jesus.

Do you want to be in the school of Jesus or Satan?

Church

Church is the house of God.

That is where we worship and praise him.

We interact with other believers of God there.

All of us believers of God are a church family.

We all are brothers and sisters of Gods family.

The Family of God has each other's backs.

Brothers and sisters of God help one another out during hard times.

Four Seasons

All four Seasons are beautiful in their own way.

Spring is beginning of the new year.

It is colorful and slightly warm.

Summer is hot, humid, and wet.

Fall is slightly cold, and you start seeing different colors in the leaves.

As they start coming down slowly one by one at a time.

Winter is very cold, wet, and very slippery.

This is how our life with Jesus goes.

It is an exceptionally long cycle we must go through to grow in Jesus.

Moon

We are as a moon fighting the devil in sleep mode.

The devil is always in attack mode twenty-four seven.

As a Christian we should be in attack mode twenty-four seven too.

In our sleep we are fighting the devil.

We are constantly at war with the devil its never-ending war with devil as a soldier of God.

What is love?

What is true pure love?

Jesus first loved us.

So, we can love ourselves and others.

I had a hard time loving myself and others

because I was not shown love for a long time.

So, what is love like?

How do we show love?

I am learning how to love show love.

People have showed me love from time to time, but I have always turned it down.

Love has always been one of my problems.

So just love me for who I am please.

We are not perfect like Jesus.

Jesus always loves us no matter what we do.

We need to show the same love Jesus has for us.

Disciples

I am a disciple of The Lord Jesus.

We are a family and crew.

He works in me for his will not mine.

I am 3 in 1: a servant, poet, and disciple for The Lord Jesus.

There is nothing more pleasant than that.

Because a disciple works is never done.

Even a disciple in training is always busy.

Be an honest and humble disciple.

We are all called to be disciples for Jesus.

Do not run from your calling.

Listen to your calling.

Treasure

Our treasure is in heaven not on Earth.

Most people think that treasure is on Earth.

A few know that the true treasure is in heaven.

That was once me at one point.

Not anymore!!

I keep on digging for that spiritual gold.

Some people dig then give up.

Do not give up on your treasure.

Fight for your treasure that belongs to you.

I am not a quitter who gives up.

That is My treasure so hands off.

I found it first buck a roo.

So get your own diamonds, gold, silver buddy.

Search real hard for your treasure and do not ever give up looking for it.

You will find it in time.

Stay faithful in heavenly treasures.

Jesus will give us treasures in his timing.

Stay off the earthly treasure.

Years

As years pass, we age.

We have all made mistakes in our lifetime.

But we learn from the mistakes we make.

I have made a lot of mistakes in my lifetime.

Now I am seeing and learning from them.

Some people just need time to learn from them.

That was for me.

I need time to learn from mine.

That is the same way for our walk with Jesus.

We make mistakes in our Christian walk, but we also learn from those mistakes.

Jesus will help us learn from all our mistakes.

He is always there for us no matter what we do.

There is always true pure love.

Love and hope are the two greatest gifts there is.

That means everything to me from the bottom of my heart.

It will always be till my last breath on this earth.

Art Forms

There are many art forms in this world.

There is cooking, drawing, and writing.

Writing comes in many different forms.

We have poetry, stories, and music.

There is many other art forms out there.

My art form is poetry.

All art forms start as an idea.

Ideas always start in the mind.

The Holy Spirit gives me my ideas.

How do you use your ideas?

Do you use them for yourself or for Jesus?

I use mine for The Lord Jesus all the way.

What are your ideas and art forms?

Use them in the right way please.

Motorcycles

There are new Christians on fire for Jesus.

That is me still.

We have a totally changed heart.

There is brand new spark plugs in us.

The old one is taken out.

We have new spiritual oil and the whole nine yards.

It is our job to maintain our spiritual motorcycles.

As we mature in Christ we can turn into muscle cars.

Then we get more and more spiritual horsepower from Jesus.

That drives us more for his will and less for ours.

He is the power and strength to our spiritual vehicles.

The holy spirit is the key to the engine.

God lights are headlights.

Through this dark and lonely empty world of sin.

Nations

The nations I am talking about is building followers of Jesus.

Not earthly nations we have.

We are to build and rise nations up from the ground.

For the kingdom of peace.

I was doing it so long for the kingdom of Darkness.

Now I am doing it for the kingdom of light.

Most people would rather create nations of Satan.

A few people want to create nations of Jesus.

Jesus nations will always overthrow Satan nations.

So, go operation "Nations Jesus" forever.

History

The mind is the biggest history bank there is.

It is also the most powerful history bank.

More powerful then a computer history bank.

It stores all that we read and listen too.

And some of our good and bad memories are there.

That is our history.

The Lord Jesus is the only one who can clean it out.

I am letting him clean out mine because it was all dirty and filthy.

We must let him come into the bank.

A lot of people do not want him coming in.

They do not want Jesus mind set and thinking.

The mind is the history bank of our life.

I'm Me

First thing is first, do not tell me how to be me!

That really gets on my nerves.

I will be me no matter what.

You do not know me.

My flow is gentle and easy.

Till you get to know me.

I am a wild white boy.

My wild is a fun one.

There are many things people do not know about me.

My sense of humor is an extremely unique one.

I am a very chill person, and easy going too.

My feelings are super sensitive.

Especially towards females the most.

Females are my weak spot.

So do not let anyone tell you how to be you.

I am young, wild, and free.

I will speak my mind.

Sea

My flow is like a smooth Pacific Ocean because it is the only calm sea.

Jesus has calmed down my sea.

Before the seas were untamable.

The Father, Jesus, and The Holy Spirit help keep my sea under control.

A flow is a smooth current of spiritual water in me.

There are two types of spiritual water in me.

They are smooth and rough.

The smooth flow comes from The Lord Jesus, and the rough flow comes from the devil.

You can have your sea controlled by Jesus or Satan.

I would rather have my flow be spiritual sea controlled by Jesus.

Then my flow moves along a lot easier.

Original Sin

Original sin took place in the garden of Eden.

This is where all sickness and disease came from.

It affected the rest of the seed from Adam and Eve.

They messed up big time by disobeying God.

That is why we all have a sinful nature.

Jesus came as the second Adam to set us free.

Through him we are washed away from sin.

We all still have our short comings.

Just remember Jesus paid your price on the cross.

River

As a church family we are to be on one accord.

Our primary focus is Jesus and his kingdom.

So many churches work independently or with God leading their path.

The churches are to flow like a river connected as one.

We are stronger together then separated.

Satan wants to weaken the church.

We are to stand firm on the battlefield.

Us being whole we will overthrow the kingdom of darkness.

Comedians

The greatest doctors in the world are comedians.

They cure the worst moods in people.

To me they can cure any sickness in the mind.

Our mind is where the greatest sickness is.

God gave comedians one of the best medicines in the world.

Laughter is the best medicine I have had in my life.

Jesus through the comedian can cure the mind.

Remember to have a good laugh daily.

Princes

There are two princes in this world.

There is Jesus and Satan.

Jesus is The Prince of Peace.

Satan is the prince of evil.

The prince of evil is the ruler of this world for now.

In the future The Prince of Peace will be the ruler of the world.

I once was under the prince of evil, but now I am under control of The Prince of Peace.

Which prince is controlling your life?

My life is controlled by Prince Jesus.

Internet

Gods internet is lightening fast like quick draw.

Our internet is not as fast as the flash.

Jesus' internet source is beyond our small minds.

The Holy Spirit wants to bath us in his power source.

The most powerful internet source comes from God.

Are main key to the internet is to focus on God.

Many people forget their internet source.

Other would rather go of their own internet.

For You I will

For you I will go out of my way to give a helping hand.

This is my duty as a man and servant of God.

I am the original Richie helping hand anytime.

Having a ministering helping heart is especially important.

My Love is an overflow of pouring raindrops.

I will cross the sea for you at any cost.

Mountains will be moved for you with my pain and drive.

A tuned in spirit and ear are essential for a Christ like lifestyle.

Love is the biggest operation tool for a child of God.

For you I will do anything that is needed.

Human Body

The temple of the lord dwells within us.

So many people think that they own their body.

We do not own it God owns it.

It is an amazing machine.

For a longtime I did not see that.

A lot of us do not see how our body works.

Half the things our body does makes me curious.

On how God created us.

This is where The Holy Spirit operates.

The human body is God's, Jesus', and The Holy Spirit's dwelling place with us.

Teachers

True teachers of the word of God are his vessels.

For instances Brother Rome is a Vessel at Kingdom Lifeline Ministries.

God's Teachers have a true relationship with him.

Teachers come in many different forms.

Some are pastors, apostles, and ministers.

There are a lot of teachers for The Kingdom of Heaven.

A teacher's job is to show and teach how to truly live as god's anointed one.

Being a teacher is a noticeably big role inside of The Kingdom of Heaven.

Maps

The biggest map for us is The Holy Bible.

Jesus guides us down the map called life.

Then there is another map called death guided by Satan.

These are the two spiritual maps of life.

Just as a map guides you to your destination our spiritual map guides us to our eternal destination.

You have Jesus the perfect map then you have Satan the evil map.

Choose your map of life smart.

My map of life is with The Lord Jesus.

Either have the map of joy or anger?

Love Language

There is a special love language between a men, women, and God.

It is a certain unique code between the two.

My love language with God is extremely special.

So, it is with Jesus.

A marriage love language is about learning your lover.

That love language is an amazing love code between a husband and a wife.

It is the tool to a marriage and to have it with Jesus.

The code of love is about quality time with each other.

Learn your lovers love language.

Mountains

There are many mountains in life.

Just like any mountain you must go up.

The spiritual mountains just keep getting harder and higher.

As they keep getting harder the stronger our faith grows.

To command those mountains out of our lives.

More mountains we move the better the view gets.

To a place with green grass and flowers.

Pouring out with overflowing rivers and waterfalls.

That is where my place of faith is with Jesus.

Relationship

What is a relationship all about?

How do we operate in one?

A relationship starts with The Lord Jesus.

He will teach us how to have a true relationship with love.

My relationship with Jesus is a huge part of my faith walk.

Because of being born in sin which throws our eyes off the big prize.

It is the most amazing bond with our Lord Jesus.

So, do not take your eyes of off the big prize Jesus.

Fight a good fight soldiers of faith.

City's

In life there is many cities.

Just like the many cities in the spirit.

They can be of good or evil spirits.

Some of the cities of Christ is love, joy, and peace.

The cities of Satan are hate, anger, and lying.

My city in the spirit of Jesus Christ.

You have the option to change your cities spirit.

It can lead to eternal life or eternal torment.

The spirit of your city will choose your destination.

Muscles

Just like our natural muscles we must exercise our spiritual muscles daily.

To get bigger, to lift our spiritual weights daily.

Like our natural muscles we need to feed them afterwards.

The same thing goes for our spiritual muscle growth.

So, we can knock the enemy right out of the ring.

Then claim the prize The Lord Jesus Christ, the most high and powerful one.

More Money More Problems

A lot of people think that money buys happiness.

You can have what the flesh desires.

Still be unhappy deep inside.

Only Jesus provides the joy and peace the heart desires.

Many rely on temporary happiness and joy.

Jesus is the everlasting source of happiness and joy.

If we keep our eyes on him, he will give whatever our hearts desire.

Constitution

A soldier for Christ constitution, The Holy Bible.

Just like the American soldiers have the US constitution.

They both give us rights and regulations to follow.

Christ soldiers must follow both constitutions.

More importantly the Biblical 1 first.

The constitution I follow guides my life right.

God's constitution has always been perfect.

Man is the one who messed up not God.

The constitution man made has some flaws.

Only God can correct the flaws in man's constitution.

Marine

I am a Jesus Christ Marine Corp Fighter.

This is not your ordinary Marine soldier.

We do not fight with physical weapons.

The weapons we use are spiritual.

We are ambassadors' marine soldiers for The Lord Jesus Christ.

Do not be afraid to fight for God's Kingdom.

Crush the enemy's kingdom and territory.

Show him who oversees our lives.

So, let us be marine soldiers of strong courage.

Remember you are not in this alone.

Jesus is right by your side everywhere you go.

Unpretty

Do not let anybody tell you you are not pretty.

God Wants all his daughters to know they are beautiful.

You are like precious jewels in his sight.

So, men show them that they are queens.

The Lord Jesus loves all his special daughters with unique gifts.

Ladies you have a heavenly father that will never let you down.

There is a comforter The Holy Spirit that is always with you.

You will always be special in The Lord Jesus sight.

Run Away

All of Jesus' true disciples have enemies.

The one with no enemies are not real disciples.

True disciples know when to run and when not to.

It is a daily learning process.

I used to be the one that would run away from everything.

Now I know when to and not to.

God's disciples listen to Jesus for handling enemies.

The Lord Jesus always has your back.

He always guides his true disciples that are true and honest with themselves.

They know how to fight their personal issues.

We may struggle sometimes but we keep fighting on.

Time After Time

Time after time you must be yourself.

We all have an inner child in us that The Lord Jesus had placed in us purposely.

In his eyes he sees us as little children.

We are children of royalty of the most high God almighty.

So, rejoice to be in the kingdom of eternal peace.

Be glad to be heirs of The Lord Jesus.

Then give praises of thanksgiving to The Lord Jesus.

So, happy Thanksgiving to everybody.

Angel of Mine

All of us have an angel God gave us.

He sends us angels at our lowest point in life.

Be grateful for the angel in your life.

Thank you, pastor Jack and Kurt, for believing in me.

For not giving up on me when I did.

I know I was a bit of work.

So, Pastor Jack and Kurt you two I am most appreciative of from the bottom of my heart.

You 2 always saw hope in me.

So, show the angel that God put in your life some appreciation.

Live your life

This life is not ours.

God gives and takes away life.

So many people live however they want.

At one point that once was me.

Just doing whatever I wanted.

Now my life is fully for The Lord Jesus.

I am still a work in progress.

All his sons and daughters are.

We are to live while serving The Lord Jesus.

He is our guide in this dark and lonely world.

This world has no place in it not without Jesus to give it light.

Life Goes On

In a true disciple walk there are some hardships.

There are disappointments and many more.

We need to know to trust in The Lord Jesus.

So we can overcome them.

It is not always easy at times.

Remember just keep that strong courageous faith.

We are soldiers of faith in Jesus' army.

So do not let the devil get in your head.

Stay strong for your Lord Jesus kingdom of peace and love.

Life goes on through good and bad times.

Meant To Be

    We all have callings that are to be fulfilled.
Our lives on earth are temporary and only a short time.

The Lord Jesus will guide you through training.

The Holy Spirit will show you how to walk it out.

All of our calling are different.

God gives all of us a unique calling.

So seek out your calling in your life.

Do not give up once you know your calling.

Stay strong through each task that is given.

Operation Jesus

Either you are for operation Jesus or operation Satan.

Both operation's eyes are on a different mission.

Lord Jesus comes to bring peace and joy.

Satan comes to bring lies and doubt.

Before I was in operation Satan.

Now I live in operation Jesus all the time.

It is a daily constant uphill battle.

So, fight a good uphill battle for the kingdom.

Those uphill battle will only make you stronger.

Remember do not give in to operation Satan.

Faith Is A Journey

Faith is the greatest journey in a person's life.

There are always new adventures to explore.

The adventures are always interesting and different.

Each day brings a more challenging adventure.

We must walk in them with childlike faith.

Faith is like relearning how to walk all over again.

To expand our faith, we have to take baby steps.

Walking with integrity is stepping out in strong faith.

A Child like faith is like a flowing current.

The Importance of Repentance

Repentance is a never-ending spiritual shower.

Just like a natural shower.

We must maintain spiritual hygiene.

Staying clean before Jesus is a process.

Repentance is like relearning how to talk all over again.

The biggest problem with most Christians is they do not know the importance of true honest repentance.

Most people do not want to maintain their spiritual hygiene.

The Spirit of Family Love

Family love is like an engine.

Love has different parts attached to it.

Just like an engine they must work together.

The spirit of love is not about flesh and blood.

It is about the unity of love in a family.

The unity of love keeps the family strong.

Love is what keeps a family together.

It is what makes a family a whole unit.

Eight Mile

This is the eight mile road of JCP.

The hurt and the pain of JCP's life story.

My first biggest hurt scared me for a long time.

Not knowing the love of the one who gave birth to you.

It was a very dark and lonely childhood.

Having an abusive dad only made things worse.

For a long time, I felt trapped inside a dark and cold closet.

As time passed by my anger became more like a bomb.

My heart became like a wall towards love.

Then an incredibly special person came into my life.

She made me feel like I was somebody.

That feeling made life worth living.

When she passed away then it went downhill.

It sparked a huge atomic bomb of anger inside me.

That is when I utterly lost all hope in everything.

Once Jesus truly came into my heart.

I found hope and love all over again.

The Lord Jesus made life worth living again.

He took out all the radiation in my heart.

Jesus told me that I am special in his sight.

This is my eight mile road in my own words.

Channel

Let us take an adventure down the channel of life.

Through the peaceful waters of faith.

Cruising along in the boat of hope.

As The Holy Spirit guides the sail of love.

Getting a spiritual tan from the light of Jesus.

So, let us find the real meaning of happiness down this channel.

Instead of going down the channel of death.

Which is guided by Satan.

To many people take the so-called easy channel.

So, find the channel of life deep within you.

Then do not ever lose sight of it in your heart.

Do not get spiritually lazy on your adventure.

Not Afraid

I am not afraid to take a fight for my life.

To overcome the deep and dark parts of myself.

Bringing your fears to the light of Christ.

To many people hide from there darkest inner fears.

That used to be me.

Being a chicken not facing them head on.

So, let us take them to the ring of love.

Knock them all out with the power of Christ in us.

It is the time to face them head on and overcome them like a man.

So, let us stop running from our fears.

Let us live the life we are meant to live.

When I needed an angel

When I needed an angel you always sent one.

Even when I did not see it.

You were always looking over me.

Even when I felt all alone like no one cared.

There was always an angel looking over me.

To all the angels in my life thank you.

You do not know how much you mean to me.

Your love kept me fighting through hard times.

Without you guys I could not have kept on going.

Beautiful America

Beautiful America was based off God's word.

That is what gives America her beauty.

The light that glows in her shining freedom.

Our freedom cost a price of painful love.

Her light is an ever-burning torch of hope.

America's beauty is the faith in Christ.

Faith is what gives America her beautiful colors.

This is what makes America a special place to be in.

So be proud to be an American.

Lose yourself

Lose yourself to the beat of the music.

Just let the flow fly freely through.

That is the flow of The Holy Spirit working through you.

The rhythm of the flow will only increase.

Faster the beat gets the harder the task.

It must stay at a constant current flow.

Like water it always needs to stay calm.

Our flow will shine like the stars.

More current your flow the better your rhythm.

Stay tuned with the rhythm of your flow.

My flow is a freestyle rhythm.

Once you find your flow just be you.

The more you use your flow.

You will feel more looser inside.

When you write your rhythm will come naturally.

Cool Kids

The real true cool kids are less noticeable.

They are truly one of a kind.

Most people do not see how gifted they are.

A lot of times they are looked as not important.

It takes a special eye to see the true cool kids.

These fake cool kids have nothing on us.

The only one you need to tell you, you are cool is Jesus.

He knows how cool you truly are.

This world does not know what cool means.

Being cool means just be yourself.

True friends have more respect for that.

Not trying to fit in with the crowd.

Special Dad In The World

Dad you mean the whole world to me you always have.

I was just not myself for a very long time.

I have always thought the divorce between you and mom was my fault for a very long time.

You have always been there for me no matter what.

I have always had a problem expressing myself in words.

There would be times I wanted to be with you, but I was to afraid you would leave me too.

I was trying to find myself because I did not know who I was.

So many times, I wanted to fit in because I was so different from others in so many ways.

You are the best dad in the whole world and always will be forever!!!!!!!!!!!!!!!!!!!!!!!

I have messed up so many times.

We both have made a lot of mistakes.

I have messed up so many times.

We have gotten into so many fights then we have gotten along.

Music Decades

There are all types of music from decades.

Each decade of music is always changing.

Every decade of music is quite different.

Just as life is like in a decade.

Each decade special in its own.

Every generation of music is constantly changing.

There are new songs continually coming out all the time.

That is what makes each decade different.

Movies decades

Each movie is always changing all the time.

We are always seeing a new movie every day.

Every movie is different from one another.

The movie style is always changing.

How the movies are always new?

What the movies viewpoint is about is always changing.

What the movie is about is always changing all the time.

TV Shows Decade

Have you ever noticed how TV shows aint the same.

They always showing new shows.

The way of the TV shows are different.

The style of the TV shows are always changing all the time.

There are continuous changes going on.

Each show is different from one another.

Decade

Our trials are like a decade.

Each trial we start comes a new one.

We experience a new decade every day.

I am slowly dealing with my trials.

Our decades are all different.

We all have some sort of trial.

What are your trials in life?

Listening

We are to listen to God.

Also, to what others are telling us.

Listening is very important in life.

If we do not listen there will be problems.

Our ears should always be focused on God.

If we do not listen to God, we will be in trouble with him.

We do not want no issue with no one at all.

Everyone wants to get along with one another.

Singing

Singing comes from the heart.

We are to sing praises to The Lord.

When we sing it is supposed to have meaning to it.

If we sing without purpose, then it is useless.

Our singing should be honoring God.

It should not be honoring man.

Singing is a gift from God The Father.

All of us should sing praise to The Lord God Almighty.

Technology

Technology is always changing every day.

God is technology that never changes at all.

He is the same today, tomorrow, and forever.

Man made technology is always changing.

We have smart phones, tablets, and computerized watches.

It will never stop changing, never ever stop.

God is always the same.

Technology could be good or could be bad.

Faith

Faith is the biggest part of a Christian walk.

All we need is a grain of mustard seed of faith.

With faith our prayers get answered from God in time.

Faith in a Christian walk is very important.

We are to exercise that seed of faith.

It gives us trust in The Lord God Almighty.

We can do all things through him.

He is mighty and powerful.

Patience

We are to have patience in our walk with God.

Patience will get us far in our lives.

An impatient person will not get very far in life.

Patience will help you grow in The Lord Jesus Christ.

Remember to have patience throughout all time

Prayer

Prayer is talking to God Almighty The Creator.

We come to him in prayer for all our needs.

When you pray you are building a bond with him.

It really works when you put your faith into it.

We are to build a prayer alter everywhere we go.

God wants us to talk to him.

We are to pray for others and ourselves.

Purpose

God gave all his children in life purpose.

My purpose is poetry for his glory not mine.

We are to use our purpose not to let it sit.

When we get to heaven our purpose gas tank is to be empty not full.

The problem is a lot of people do not use there purpose.

What is your purpose in life?

God's plan for our lives is to use our purpose for his glory.

If you truly do not know Jesus, then you do not know purpose in life.

We all have a calling in life find yours.

Time

Men run all the time every day.

God's time is different than man's time.

Time with God is when ever and time with man is nonstop.

Jesus does not run out of time like man does.

He made time to worship, praise, and honor him.

We are to make time for The Lord our God.

People make excuses saying I do not have time for God.

Like I am to busy working grave yard shift.

Communion

Communion is the covenant of The New Testament.

We do this in remembrance of Jesus dyeing on the cross for our sins.

The wine is the blood, and the bread is the body.

As a Christian we should do this in remembrance of Jesus dying on the cross for us.

Theories

God has no theories at all.

Some people think God is all about theories.

Man has a lot of theories.

They have evolution and many more.

Like we took form from apes.

It is a lie.

All theories are big big fat lies.

Do not listen to man's theories listen to the word of God.

Toughness

True toughness is being a Christian.

A Christian is the toughest person in the world.

He is our shield that makes us tough against evil.

The unsaved think they are tough.

Satan thinks he is all big and bad.

God is wiser and smarter than the devil is.

Jesus makes us tough and strong through him.

Keep in mind true toughness comes through The Lord Jesus.

Challenges

We all have challenges in life.

They can be really hard.

You must fight through no matter what.

Do not quite through your challenges.

Your challenges will make you stronger.

Challenges will always come your way no matter what.

Face your challenge like a man and do not run from them.

Nature

We have 2 natures our new nature and our old nature.

Our new nature is in Jesus, and our old nature is in Sin.

Some people think we only have one nature.

Everyone can have 2 natures if they want too.

It is better to have a nicer nature inside of us.

Keep in mind you can have 2 natures.

Two Face

A 2 faced person is someone who goes to church and acts different when they leave.

People like that are not true believers.

They say they believe but they do not.

They are setting a bad example for others.

So do not follow their role setting.

Life lessons

A lot of people have taught a lot of life lessons.

I thank everyone that had taught me a life lesson.

It has took me a long time to appreciate them.

For a long time I was taking advantage of them.

I was not using those life lessons.

Half the time I thought people were just being mean to me or picking on me.

These life lessons have gotten me to where I am today.

So thank you once again for the life lessons you have taught me.

Rebellion

I use to have a lot of rebellion inside of me.

There would be so many time I felt rebellious.

That is one of the devil strategies to keep us in sin.

I am one of the people that had it badly.

It is a struggle to overcome it on your own.

Only through God you can overcome rebellion.

Do not try it on your own it will not work.

Bully

There are many bullies in the world.

But the biggest bully is the devil and his demons.

They are out bullying people every day.

They are the biggest bullies out there.

I have been bullied so many times before.

A bully is someone who does not feel good about themselves.

So they have to bully some one else to make themselves feel better.

Distractions

The devil is good at distractions.

That is his specialty he does.

There is a whole lot of distractions in the world.

The devil will try anything to try and distract you.

We must have our eyes opens always for signs of the devil.

Keep your eyes on that all the time.

Deeds

There are 2 deeds we can do.

Those are the devil's deeds or God's deeds.

We have to choose what deeds we want to follow.

The devil's deeds lead to death.

Lord Jesus' deeds lead to life.

Our deeds will lead us to certain places in our life.

Books

You know how you read a book you love.

Well there are 2 books in heaven.

They are the books of life and the book of judgment.

The Book of life is for the saved.

The book of judgement is for the unsaved.

Our life is like a good nonfiction story.

How people live is written in one of the 2 books.

Those books determine where we will spend eternity.

Movies

Do You love watching movies of all kinds?

Well our life is played out like a movie.

You have got action, drama, love, and humor movies.

The movie of life is all of those is one.

Our movie is one long movie about life.

Picture watching your life on a screen.

I could see my movie of life in heaven.

You can too.

Movies can be entertaining and interesting.

So, are you interested in the movie of life?

Instruments

God gave 3 instruments to us.

Those are the ears, hands, and mouth.

The ears are to listen to the word, God, and sermons.

Hand are to worship God and play earthly instruments for his glory.

Last of all the mouth is for praise and sermons.

Well also need these instruments to help other people in need.

They are not for evil use.

Lyrics

Our lyrics all come from the Bible.

We learn them by reading them daily.

The lyrics are very important.

They bring us closer to The Lord.

The words of God are like lyrics.

Those words of God give us his knowledge and wisdom.

Home

I have 2 homes Joliet and Heaven.

Home is the comfort and feeling you have.

Joliet is home because of family.

Also, the comfort and feeling of home.

You make the city or town or suburb home.

The places itself does not make it home.

My second home is heaven.

I made Joliet my home a long time ago.

Scripts

As an actor practices their scripts or a movie.

We practice our scripts for The Lord.

Our scripts are the words of God.

We need to be ready at any time.

Remembering verses are a part of the scripts in life.

Having our scripts will help us grow stronger.

Teaching other scripts is important too.

Picture yourself remembering a script for a movie you like.

Stories

There are so many stories in the Bible.

As reading a good story you pay attention.

The Bible has the best stories ever.

Bible stories are all true stories.

They teach and educate you about God.

It helps you grow stronger in The Lord God.

Those stories inspire us for life.

The Bible has the most interesting stories ever written.

The Bible is the best love story ever and the bloodiest.

Styles

There are so many styles in this world.

We have singing, rapping, hair, preaching styles and many more.

Each style is special in their own way.

All of us have our own special style.

Like I have my poetry and learning style.

Styles give us our own special characteristics.

God gave all of us different special styles for a reason.

Poetry

Poetry is an art form and a language.

This is a special type of art form.

It comes form the heart not like the mind.

The mind is (unclear) and the heart is the engine.

When you write it people have to feel it.

Poems are short stories.

You want to get the people's attention.

It is another way to tell someone what is on your mind.

Poetry is my way of expressing my feelings and what is on my mind.

It involves constant ideas all the time.

Part of poetry is observing everything around you.

Feel Me flow

Feel me flow.

Let me flow.

Flow with the Holy Spirit.

Feel me flow with the water of life.

I am like a flowing river of holy water.

My flow touches the whole world and nations.

The flow I have is relaxing and funny.

You can feel and sense me for miles away.

I have a very strong flow on me.

A flow is a strong current.

The Holy Spirit guides my flow forever.

My flow of living water sets me free.

The flow of living water comes from Jesus.

The flow of living water tells me who I am.

I have a spiritual flow inside.

A spiritual flow is better.

Let my flow touch your flow every time.

My flow touches the heart and soul.

The flow I have will help guide you.

Jesus's flow guides my flow everyday.

River of life strengthens my flow.

Holy spirit touches my flow all the time.

My flow is for everyone listening.

Bald Eagle

The bald eagle and statue of liberty is our symbol of freedom.

Just as Jesus is a Christian symbol of freedom.

We have soldiers fighting for our freedom.

I have family in the army so I know how it is.

We have true freedom through Jesus.

Thank you for fighting for my freedom Uncle Graham.

You have all my respect.

Jesus fought for us on the cross.

Nascar

I picture a walk with God like nascar.

Nascar is a fast intense high speed race.

The game is to win the race.

My walk with God is a spiritual nascar.

Racing nascar is how I see my walk with Jesus.

This image helps us stay strong in Jesus.

Jesus is the engine of my race car.

The Holy Spirit is the fuel for the car.

I am the race car.

God is the driver of my race with Jesus.

My walk in Jesus is a nascar race.

I am to win the race hard and strong.

Responsibility

Responsibility is about doing things with out being told.

It is about what needs to be done.

Part of responsibility is manning up.

This is a part of growing up.

When you are responsible you are trustworthy.

A responsible person will get very far in life.

Non responsible person will not get very far in life.

Responsibility is some thing you will learn through out life.

I am finding myself more responsible then before.

Life

Life is a very precious gift from God.

He breathes life in to us.

A lot of people don't know how special life is.

The simple things in life are the best things.

I enjoy the simple things in life.

This makes things a lot easier for you.

Some people make life very complicated.

My life is becoming more enjoyable then ever before.

Life is about living every moment, hour, and minute.

Living is going the fullest length you can reach.

It is not about always complaining everyday, or mourning.

Life is too short.

You should take a voyage like it is laid out.

Most people think of life being complicated.

Very few people think of life being simple.

I am in the second category.

I can not stress enough how very special life is.

Some people are grateful for the gift life like me.

Many people abuse the gift of life.

Life and purpose falls in place together.

Many people do not know what it is to do with the gift of life.

It is an incredibly special blessing from

The Lord God Almighty.

Rewards

Oscar rewards are for actors with movies.

Grammy awards are for music artists.

Heaven is a reward for the true Christian.

We have so many awards to get.

Rewards come in so many ways.

When you do things right or good you get rewarded.

Us Christians are always getting rewarded.

We are continuously getting rewarded.

The greatest rewards are up in heaven.

Basketball

Our live is a game of basketball.

What is living all about.

Is it about just existing in the world?

No living is about teaching the word of God.

Its showing that you care about others.

You have another way to truly live this isn't about just existing.

We are to help change the world.

Our mission is to make disciples for the lord Jesus.

Sometimes we mess up along the way.

When the time stops the game is over.

What is life meaning for people?

My lifes meaning is to fulfill my purpose.

Construction

When I think of construction I see myself.

We are all under construction of Jesus.

Like building a strong foundation.

Jesus helps build a strong foundation in us.

We are a walking construction site in progress.

It is non stop construction inside of us daily.

He can work on you to if you let him.

We are under spiritual construction for the kingdom of heaven.

Or you can be under the construction of the kingdom of darkness.

Which construction site do you want to be under the work of.

Monster Truck

We all have a spiritual monster truck in us.

You may not know you have one.

We can use it to destroy the enemy or against Jesus.

How we use it can affect others and ourselves.

A few want to learn how to use it for Jesus.

More would rather use it for Satan.

My monster truck is for team Jesus only.

What team is your monster truck working for.

I am in operation Jesus monster truck action mode.

Go monster truck Jesus to the end.

Muscle Cars

A mature Christian is like a muscle car.

There fast, powerful, and loud.

The are so much fun to drive.

God powers the muscle car with spiritual nitres gas.

It makes the person stronger.

Just like a car needs fuel we need fuel too.

Jesus is our fuel for the gift of life forever.

He moves the car for us every time we get closer.

Over drive

Over drive is to strive hard for The Lord Jesus.

A few push harder for Jesus.

More push harder for the father of lies.

They would believe lies instead

I am in God mode for life.

Jesus wants to keep us in God mode for eternity.

God mode is going to the extreme level.

Some people can not handle the extreme level.

Then there is the extreme extreme level of the God mode.

Death

There are 2 types of death.

We have spiritual and physical death.

I was once in spiritual death at one point.

You may think there is no spiritual death.

Spiritual death is very real.

So many people would rather stay in spiritual death.

Why they stay there is because of its comfort level for help.

The ones who ask for help shall be rewarded.

Those that stay in spiritual death will be punished.

Many people do not they are in spiritual death.

But there is a way out of spiritual death.

Eagle Eye

God has an eagle eye on his children all the time.

Just as parents have an eagle eye on their kids.

He cares enough about us to always be watching us.

Keeping us safe from the enemy attacks.

There are 2 big eyes always around us.

You can not see them but they are there.

Only we can see them protecting us.

No one else can see them because they are spiritual eyes.

They are unseen to the natural eye.

Driver

For a long time I was getting in the way of Jesus.

I use to think I was the driver.

We are not the driver Jesus is and always will be.

Jesus will lead our path or us.

We just have to follow the path he gives us.

Sometimes we want to get back in the driver seat and take over.

I have to daily remind myself that Jesus is the driver not me.

You need to do the same thing for yourself.

We are never ever in control from the start.

Animals

Animals are ment to be loved to.

They are also Gods creation that he made.

We also are animals in some sort of way.

So many people mistreat and abuse animals.

They want to be loved the same as we do.

Animals have feelings just like we do.

Anything that walks also hurts and has pain.

All of God's creations are very special.

Rain

There are 2 types of rain.

There is the rain of life and death.

So many people stay in the rain of death.

Few come in to rain of life.

I once was in the the rain of death.

Now I am in the rain of life, truly living.

My dad is slowly coming to the rain of life with me.

A lot of people I know are in the rain of death.

The rain of life is pure and clean.

The rain of death is dirty from sin.

God can clean that dirty rain if you let him.

Purified holy rain cleans us from dirty rain.

Many people would rather stay in unpurified rain.

Why there is no process of change at all.

Those in the purified rain are willing to go through the process of change.

No one said the process of change was going to be an easy road.

So many people want change but they are not willing to go through the process of change.

Because they say its hard and to difficult to deal with.

Fire

We can use 2 fires natural or spiritual.

So many use the natural fire against us.

Thinking it will tear and break us down.

My fire can crush and destroy at any moment or time.

Us Christians always have a steady spiritual fire that is always burning.

The natural fire will burn out after a while.

Spiritual fire will always over throw the natural fire every time.

God is the spiritual fire Satan is the natural fire.

My spiritual fire is always ready for a new battle everyday.

You have no more control over me natural fire.

Always fight your battles with a strong spiritual fire that never burns out.

Sky

The sky is very big just like God.

He is bigger then our tiny minds can think.

Sky and clouds are beautiful to look at.

Just as his mind is an amazing craft.

The sky is the best craft on earth one of them.

It surprises me how crafty God is.

And how crafty my mind is.

A crafty mind is very powerful tool.

Satan has a crafty mind too.

But Gods mind is more then the devil mind.

Our mind is to be the second most crafty there is.

It can be used for good or evil.

COLORS

Colors brighten up the day.

No colors are dull and boring.

Jesus is our colors for the wall.

Satan has no color on the wall.

My wall is more beautiful then before.

It used to be a very ugly wall.

This is a spiritual wall im talking about.

It is not a physical wall not what I am talking about.

The wall I mean is a wall of faith.

More faith and trust we have the more colors added.

Less faith the darker the wall gets.

Racism

Racism is a evil spirit from satan.

It is to keep people separated.

This has been around for many years.

That is the biggest problem today.

There are many forms of racism.

Many people think there is nothing wrong with it.

There is a huge problem with it.

So many people do stupid stuff because of it.

It is a big affect on the world today.

I am not racist at all.

As long as you respect me we are tight.

Remember racism can affect people big time.

For example Hitler and many more.

It doesn't matter on race or color.

Judging

Many of us are quick to judge others.

But we can not first judge our selves.

Only God can judge us.

The devil wants us to judge others for his glory.

God will judge us for his glory.

So many of us think we are God.

We are not God we are his creation.

Many people get so full of themselves.

That they forget who does all the judging.

It is not us who does the judging.

So many times we want all the glory.

Judges

We have 2 judges in the universe.

A spiritual judge and a earthly judge.

The spiritual judge is God.

Earthly judge is man kind.

Man kind judge is all about the money.

God is all about love and mercy.

Some earthly judges will show you grace and mercy.

Most of them are hard to the bone.

God is the best judge ever.

I would rather be judged by God then mankind.

Good vs. Better

We can do things good but we can do better.

More importantly the will of Jesus.

Those things can totally be done better.

Many people would rather stay on good.

Because that is the easy level.

A few come to the hard level.

Not many want to come to the challenging stage.

God wants us to come to the hard level.

Not stay at the easy level.

He wants us to challenge our selves.

Authority

We have authority through The Lord Jesus.

You may think you have authority on your own.

But you do not at all.

Jesus gives us the authority.

He is the main one in authority.

We are the second one in authority.

Some people abuse there authority position.

I do not abuse my authority position.

Many people can not handle authority from other people.

That was once me at one point in my life.

Thank you Jesus for authority in my life.

Paintings

There are painting in our heads.

Those are the images that comes in your head.

Most of these paintings are evil that comes to the head.

A few are good paintings.

We have to try and control those paintings.

It is not a easy to do.

We really need to fight off those evil images.

With Jesus help we can crush those evil paintings.

Jesus will replace the evil ones with pure ones.

We need to give the devil the boot and kick him out of the house.

In the Lord Jesus Name.

Dreams

Dreams are the most amazing thing ever.

God speaks to us through our dreams.

We can have good dreams or bad dreams.

Good dreams come from God.

Bad dreams come from the devil.

Jesus can give us a vision in our dreams.

Satan tries to scare us in night mares.

The devil wants to get us away from God.

God wants to draw us closer to him each day.

So be careful of your dreams.